BARRE CHORDS

By Troy Stetina

ISBN 978-0-7935-9787-1

HAL•LEONARD® CORPORATION

7777 W. BLUEMOUND RD. P.O. BOX 13819 MILWAUKEE, WI 53213

Visit Hal Leonard Online at
www.halleonard.com

The Author

Troy Stetina is an internationally recognized guitarist and educator, with over twenty instructional methods to his credit. He is also a contributing writer for *GuitarOne* magazine and operates his recording studio, "Artist Underground," in Milwaukee, Wisconsin. Formerly Director of Rock Guitar at the Wisconsin Conservatory of Music, Troy has created university-level programs and continues to teach master classes and performance workshops around the country. His debut instrumental guitar CD *Exottica* is available on ModRock Records. Visit Troy online at:

www.stetina.com
www.modrock.com

Other instructional products by Troy Stetina:

Metal Lead Guitar Primer
Metal Lead Guitar Volumes 1 & 2
Speed Mechanics for Lead Guitar
Metal Rhythm Guitar Volumes 1 & 2
Thrash Guitar Method
Heavy Metal Guitar Tricks
Secrets to Writing Killer Metal Songs
Speed and Thrash Drum Method
Beginning Rock Lead Guitar pocket guide
Beginning Rock Lead Guitar video
Beginning Rock Rhythm Guitar pocket guide
Beginning Rock Rhythm Guitar video
'90s Acoustic Rock
New Rock
Funk Rock
Hard Rock
Left-Handed Guitar—The Complete Method
Best of Black Sabbath—Signature Licks
The Ultimate Scale Book
Total Rock Guitar

Barre Chords
The Ultimate Method and Reference Guide

by Troy Stetina

CONTENTS

Introduction

The term "barre" is just the Spanish spelling of the English word "bar." The Spanish spelling was adopted into general guitar terminology probably due to the prevalent use of the barring technique in flamenco guitar music. Now, however, it is widely employed in virutually all guitar styles.

A barre is simply one finger placed across the strings in order to fret two or more strings. This technique allows open chord shapes to be transformed into movable barre chords and opens up a whole new dimension to guitar playing.

Two Sides of the Coin

Chords have two different aspects, like the two sides of a coin. One aspect is the *root note* on which the chord is built. This gives the chord its letter name.

The other aspect is the *type of chord*, which is determined by the relative structure of the other notes based upon that root note.

So, for example, if a major chord was built upon root note C, the resulting chord is a C major chord. Built upon G♭, it is a G♭ major chord. Build a minor structure upon the root C and you have a C minor chord. The point is that these two aspects—root and chord-type—are independent and separate from one another.

Reading Chord Diagrams

The diagrams used throughout this book depict small sections of the fretboard. The strings are represented by vertical lines, and the frets by horizontal lines. Dots on the grid show where to put your fingers. A curved line indicates that a barre is employed, where one finger lays flat to fret two or more strings. A fret number to the right of the diagram means that the diagram represents a higher section of the neck, beginning at the fret indicated.

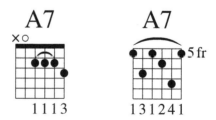

An "x" above a string means that it is not played. An unfilled "o" above a string means it is played open. Numbers across the bottom show which finger to use on each string. The left hand fingers are numbered, index finger = 1, middle finger = 2, ring finger = 3, and pinky = 4. If the thumb is employed (by reaching over the top of the neck), it will be indicated by the letter "T."

How to Use this Book

This book can function as a reference, in which you look up a particular chord and learn its shape as needed, but it is also structured as a "chord method." That is, if you start at the beginning and learn the chord shapes in the order presented, you will find that they build in a logical and systematic sequence.

Learning these chords is a process that will take some time and practice. Don't pressure yourself to learn them too quickly, as this will only cause you to confuse one with the next. Take your time. Beyond that bit of advice, there is the ever-present usage factor. That is, the best way to memorzie these new chord shapes is to *use them in music that you play*.

For that reason, sample progressions are included in the book. But this is just the starting point. Dig up more music examples that use the same types of chords and learn them. If this is difficult to find, it may be very beneficial for you to seek out private lessons with a teacher who can help you find appropriate real-world musical applications for each chord type. This is particularly important because the examples shown in this book tend to dwell upon the single shape in question, whereas in musical situations, the chord types are often mixed.

Movable Shapes and Roots

In this book, each chord type is shown as movable shapes. Since it would be redundant to literally show twelve of each shape on consecutive frets (to cover each letter name), each movable shape is shown only once and a diagram of all the note names on the neck appears at the end of the book on page 47. To play any chord type as a specific letter-named chord (i.e., A major, Cadd9, E7♭9, etc.), simply slide the appropriate chord shape for that type of chord up or down the neck to place its root on the correct letter name for that string. After you see a few sample progressions, this will be a piece of cake.

Stylistic Considerations

Chords are to a certain extent style-specific. For example, straight major and minor chords are commonly found in rock and pop styles. The heavier rock and metal styles tend to favor power chords. Seventh and Ninth chords are often found in blues and jazz. The extended chords and more complex altered chords tend to be the exclusive province of jazz.

Although you may not be primarily interested in all these styles, I would encourage you to strive for a least a basic understanding of the more complex chord types because this will enhance your overall understanding of the guitar and the fretboard.

PART I
Major & Minor Chords

MAJOR

Major chords are the starting point for any in-depth chord analysis. They have a strong and bright, or happy quality and always consist of a root note, a major 3rd tone, and a perfect 5th tone—known in terms of scale steps as the *chord formula* 1-3-5.

Major: 1–3–5

There are five movable major shapes, derived from the five open chords: E, A, D, C, and G. Each movable shape can be used to play any letter-named chord.

Major, E-form

The *E-form* major chord shape is so-named because it resembles the shape of the open E major chord. Play the open E below using fingers 2, 3, and 4 (so your index finger is available). Then slide everything up one fret and use your free index finger to barre all six strings at the first fret. You are now playing an F major barre chord (using the E-form movable shape).

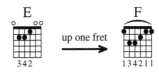

The root of this chord shape lies on the low sixth string and is represented by the circled dot in the diagram below. Slide the entire shape up or down the neck, placing this dot on any letter named note, and you can play a major chord by that name. Remember, don't confuse "E-form" with an E chord. The "form" only indicates that it has a *shape* similar to that of an open E chord. Again, this movable form may be used to play *any* letter-named major chord.

Movable E-form

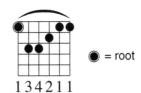

⦿ = root

1 3 4 2 1 1

> • If this chord shape is new to you, it may take some time to master. Pick each string of the chord one at a time and work on eliminating any dead or "buzzing" strings.

For a diagram displaying all the note names on the sixth string, see page 47. At this point, it would be wise to memorize the note names on the sixth string of the guitar, if you don't already know them.

The following chord progressions use full E-form major barre chords. Feel free to improvise different strumming-type rhythms.

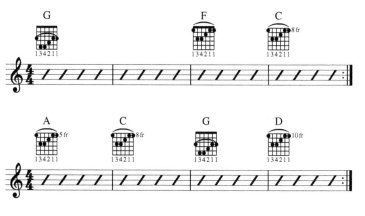

Smaller portions of the full shape are sometimes used. These are called *partial barre chords*. As long as they contain the three notes that make up the root, major 3rd, and 5th, these partial shapes are still complete major chords.

Common partial shapes of the E-form barre chord utilize strings 1-4 and 2-5. These are used in the progressions below.

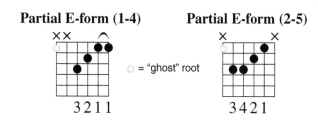

Partial E-form (1-4)   **Partial E-form (2-5)**

○ = "ghost" root

3 2 1 1   3 4 2 1

- Envision the full chord shape from which these partial shapes are drawn, even though you are only playing a smaller piece of it. In particular, pay attention to the location of the unplayed "ghost" root on the sixth string which names each chord.

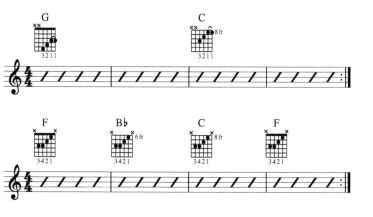

Other possible partial E-form shapes use strings 1-3, 2-4, and 3-5. Play the above progressions again, substituting these partial shapes. Then try to create a few more progressions of your own.

Major, A-form

The *A-form* chord shape is so-named because it resembles the shape of the open A chord. Play the open A below using your third finger as a barre (so your index finger is available). Then slide everything up one fret and use your free index finger to fret the string 5 at the first fret. You are now playing a B♭ major barre chord (using the A-form movable shape).

The root of this chord shape lies on the fifth string and is represented by the circled dot in the diagram below. Slide the entire shape up or down the neck, placing this dot on any letter named note, and you can play a major chord by that name. Don't confuse "A-form" with an A chord. The "form" only indicates that it has a *shape* similar to that of an open A chord. This movable form may be used to play *any* letter-named major chord.

Movable A-form

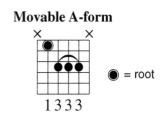

⊙ = root

1 3 3 3

The following chord progression uses A-form major barre chords. Improvise different strumming-type rhythms.

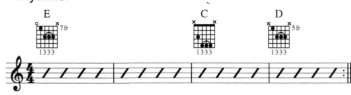

A common partial shape of the A-form omits the root note, using strings 2-4. Another adds the first string. In each case, envision the full chord shape and pay special attention to the location of the "ghost" root.

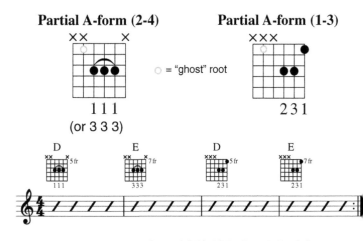

Partial A-form (2-4)   Partial A-form (1-3)

○ = "ghost" root

• At this point it is recommended that you now memorize the letter names of the notes on the fifth string. See page 47.

Major, D-form

The *D-form* chord shape is so-named because it resembles the shape of the open D chord. Play the open D below using fingers 2, 3, and 4 (so your index finger is available). Then slide everything up one fret and use your free index finger to fret string 5 at the first fret. You are now playing an E♭ major barre chord (using the D-form movable shape).

The root of this chord shape lies on the fourth string and is represented by the circled dot in the diagram below. Slide the entire shape up or down the neck, placing this dot on any letter named note, and you can play a major chord by that name.

Movable D-form

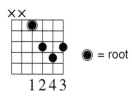

The full D-form major shape is fairly cumbersome so it is rarely used. However, you should still be aware of the full shape as it is the source of the commonly used partial shape shown below. Practice the following chord progression using full D-form major chords.

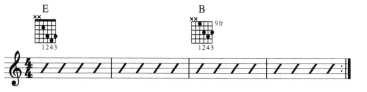

The common partial shape of the D-form barre chord simply omits the root note and utilizes strings 1-3. Again, envision the full chord shape and pay attention to the location of the "ghost" root.

Partial D-form (1-3)

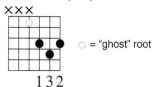

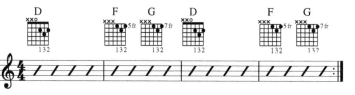

• At this point it is recommended that you now memorize the letter names of the notes on the fourth string. See page 47.

Major, C-form

The *C-form* chord shape is so-named because it resembles the shape of the open C chord. Play the open C below using fingers 2, 3, and 4 (so the index finger is available). Then slide everything up one fret and use your free index finger to barre strings 1 and 3 at the first fret. You are now playing a D♭ major barre chord (using the C-form movable shape).

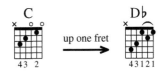

The root of this chord shape lies on the fifth string and is represented by the circled dot in the diagram below. Slide the entire shape up or down the neck, placing this dot on any letter named note, and you can play a major chord by that name.

Movable C-form

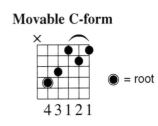

◉ = root

Because this shape is fairly cumbersome, it is rarely used in its entirety. However, you should still be aware of the full barre-chord shape. Practice the chord progression below using full C-form barre chords.

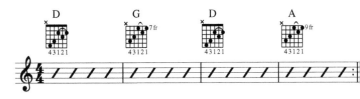

The more common partial shapes of the C-form barre chord are shown below. Envision the full chord shape and pay attention to the location of the "ghost" root.

Partial C-form (1-4)   **Partial C-form (2-4)**

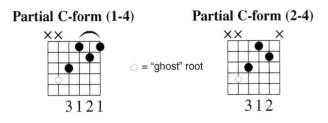

○ = "ghost" root

This following progression uses both partial shapes. Notice the move from the A-form to the C-form. For this, leave your index finger in place, barring at the fifth fret, throughout measures 3 and 4.

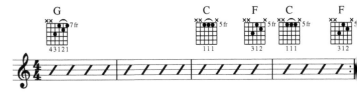

Major, G-form

The *G-form* chord shape is so-named because it resembles the shape of the open G chord. Play the open G below using fingers 2, 3, and 4 (so your index finger is available). Then slide everything up one fret and use your free index finger to barre strings 2-4 at the first fret. You are now playing an A♭ major barre chord (using the G-form movable shape).

The root of this chord shape lies on the low sixth string and is represented by the circled dot in the diagram below. Slide the entire shape up or down the neck, placing this dot on any letter named note, and you can play a major chord by that name.

Movable G-form

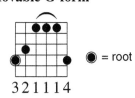

3 2 1 1 1 4

 = root

The G-form major shape is particularly difficult, and so is rarely if ever used in full—it's more of a theoretical chord shape. Nevertheless, envision the full chord shape and pay attention to the location of the "ghost" root as you play these two partial shapes.

Partial G-form (1-4)   **Partial G-form (2-5)**

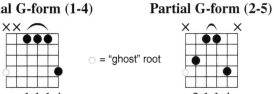

1 1 1 4   ○ = "ghost" root   3 1 1 4

- Partial G-form using strings 2-5 happens to have the third tone of the chord as the lowest-sounding note. Therefore, it is known as a *first inversion* major chord. (The same is true for the partial C-forms on the previous page, as well.) Inverted chords are sometimes written as "slash chords." For example, the first C below could also be written as C/E (read "C over E").

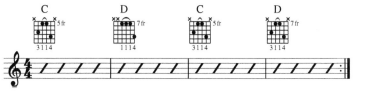

- The astute guitarist may notice that all five forms (E-form, A-form, D-form, G-form, and C-form) are interconnected on the fretboard. Try playing five different E chords, for example, using each of the five forms to see this occur.

Minor chords have a sad or delicate flavor, and consist of a root note, a minor (flatted) 3rd, and a perfect 5th. The *chord formula* is 1–♭3–5.

$$\text{Minor: } 1\text{–}\flat3\text{–}5$$

There are five movable minor shapes, parallel to the five major shapes shown previously. Each movable shape can be used to play any letter-named chord.

Minor, E-form

The *minor E-form* barre chord resembles the shape of the open E minor chord in exactly the same way as the major form did, back on page 6. The root lies on the low sixth string. Slide the entire shape up or down the neck, placing the root on any letter named note, and you can play a minor chord by that letter name.

Movable Minor E-form

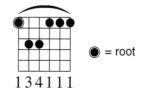

⬤ = root

1 3 4 1 1 1

The sample progression below uses minor E-form chords. Memorize the note names on the sixth string now, if you don't already know them. See page 47.

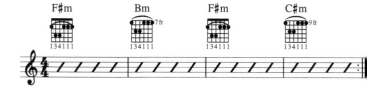

F#m	Bm	F#m	C#m
134111	7 fr 134111	134111	9 fr 134111

A common partial shape of the Em-form barre chord utilizes strings 1-4. Another uses strings 1-3 and adds the low sixth string, muting the fourth and fifth strings in between. Now try playing the progression above using the partial minor shapes shown below

.
- Pay special attention to the location of the "ghost" root and envision the full chord shape as you play the partials.

Partial Em-form (1-4)   **Partial Em-form (1-3, 6)**

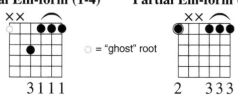

○ = "ghost" root

3 1 1 1   2   3 3 3

Other possible partial Em-form shapes use strings 1-3 and 2-5. Try the above progression again with these partial shapes as well.

Minor, A-form

The *minor A-form* barre chord resembles the shape of the open Am chord just as the major form did back on page 8. The root lies on the fifth string. Slide the entire shape up or down the neck, placing the root on any letter named note, and you can play a minor chord by that letter name.

Movable Minor A-form

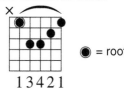

1 3 4 2 1

○ = root

Try the following progression with full minor A-form chords. Then play it again using the partial shapes shown below. Memorize the note names on the fifth string if you don't already know them. (See page 47.)

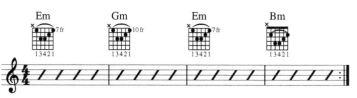

Em   Gm   Em   Bm

Partial Am-form (2-5)   **Partial Am-form (1-3)**

1 3 4 2   3 2 1

○ = "ghost" root

Minor, D-form

The *minor D-form* barre chord resembles the shape of the open Dm chord. The root lies on the fourth string. Slide the entire shape up or down the neck, placing the root on any letter named note, and you can play a minor chord by that letter name.

Movable Minor D-form

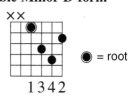

1 3 4 2

○ = root

Try the sample progression below with full minor D-form barre chords. Then try it with the partial shapes below (using Am-form partial for Am-form chords.)

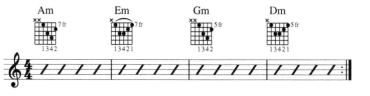

Am   Em   Gm   Dm

Partial Dm-form (1-3)   **Alt. Dm-form (1-5)**

2 3 1   1 1 3 4 2

○ = "ghost" root

13

Minor, C-form

The *minor Cm-form* barre chord doesn't actually arise from an open chord shape (there is no open Cm chord). Rather, it is simply a minor variation of the C-form. Although its full minor shape is unplayable, there are two partial versions of the full shape, which are usable. The root lies on the fifth string. Slide the entire shape up or down the neck, placing the root on any letter named note, and you can play a minor chord by that letter name.

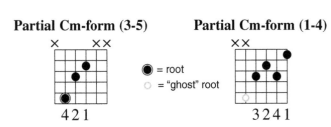

Partial Cm-form (3-5)   **Partial Cm-form (1-4)**

● = root
○ = "ghost" root

The following progression is written with the Cm-form barre chord using strings 1-4. Also substitute the other Cm-form using strings 3-5. (In this case, play the F major chord using only strings 3-5 as well.)

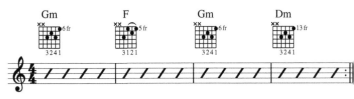

Minor, G-form

As above, the *minor G-form* barre chord also does not arise from an open chord shape (there is no open Gm chord). Rather, it is simply a minor variation on the G-form. Although its full theoretical shape is unplayable, there are several partial versions which are used. The root lies on the sixth string. Slide the entire shape up or down the neck, placing the root on any letter named note, and you can play a minor chord by that letter name.

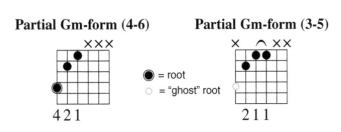

Partial Gm-form (4-6)   **Partial Gm-form (3-5)**

● = root
○ = "ghost" root

Try the sample progression below using each type of the Gm-form barre chords shown above. (When using the second form above, play the same strings 3-5 for the A major chord.)

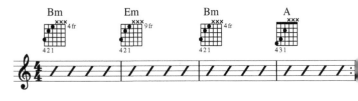

PART II
Simple Alterations

POWER CHORDS

Power chords are major or minor chords in which the 3rd tone (known as the "color tone") has been omitted. In other words, they consist of only a root note and a perfect 5th. Power chords have a "hollow-sounding" or stark quality when compared to major and minor chords, and they tend to be used prominently in the heavier rock styles. The *chord formula* is 1–5.

Power chord: 1–5

There are five movable power chord shapes, parallel to the five major shapes shown previously. Each movable shape can be used to play any letter named chord.

Power Chord, E-form

Also sometimes called "sixth-string power chords" because the root lies on string 6, *E5-form* barre chords resemble the shape of the open E5 power chord. Slide the entire shape up or down the neck, placing the root on any letter named note, and you can play a power chord by that letter name. There is a two-string and a three-string version, which simply adds an octave root. A third version omits the low root, and appears as a 4th dyad power chord shape.

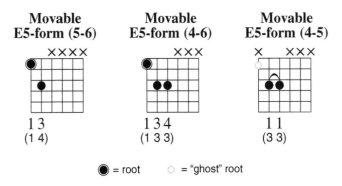

Movable E5-form (5-6)	Movable E5-form (4-6)	Movable E5-form (4-5)
1 3 (1 4)	1 3 4 (1 3 3)	1 1 (3 3)

● = root   ○ = "ghost" root

The sample progression below uses E5-form power chords. Try using each of the shapes above. Memorize the note names on the sixth string now, if you don't already know them. See page 47.

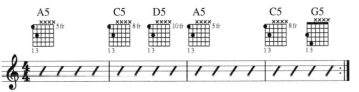

- Use the underside of your index finger to lightly touch and hold strings 1-3 muted, to eliminate unwanted string noise.

Power Chord, A-form

Also called "fifth-string power chords" because the root lies on the fifth string, *A5-form* barre chords resemble the shape of the open A5 power chord. Slide the entire shape up or down the neck, placing the root on any letter named note, and you can play a power chord by that letter name. There is a two-string and a three-string version, which adds the octave root. A third version adds the 5th in the bass, creating an inversion. Possible fourth and fifth versions would be the 4th dyad shape found on strings 3-4 and 5-6.

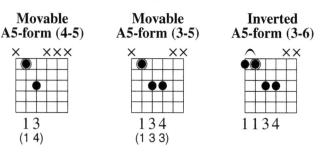

The following progression uses A5-form chords. Play it with each of the shapes shown above. Also, memorize the note names on the fifth string if you don't already know them. (See page 47.)

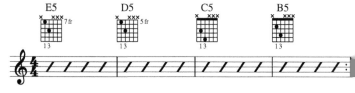

Power Chord, D-form

Also sometimes called "fourth-string power chords" because the root lies on string 4, *D5-form* chords resemble the shape of the open D5 power chord. Slide the entire shape up or down the neck, placing the root on any letter named note, and you can play a power chord by that letter name. There is a two-string and a three-string version, which adds an octave root. A third version adds the 5th in the bass, creating an inversion.

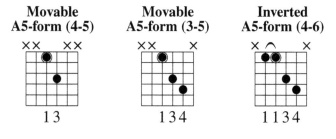

The following progression uses D5-form chords. Play it with each of the shapes shown above. Also, memorize the note names on the fourth string if you don't already know them. (See page 45.)

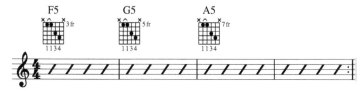

Power Chord, C-form

The *C5-form* power chord requires that an intervening string is muted. This shape is more theoretical than practical. It is more often played without the lower root note, as an upper-range 4th dyad chord using strings 2-3. (Note that this shape could also be seen as coming from the D-form.) Slide up or down the neck, placing the root on any letter named note, and you can play a power chord by that letter name.

Movable C5-form (2-3, 5)   **Partial C5-form (2-3)**

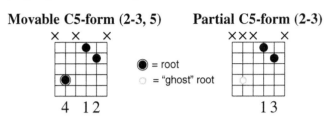

● = root
○ = "ghost" root

- Lightly touch and hold string 4 muted with the side of one of your fretting fingers, to eliminate unwanted string noise.

The following progression uses C5-form chords. Play it with each of the shapes shown above.

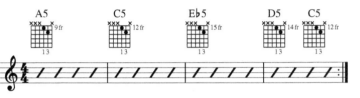

Power Chord, G5-form

The *G5-form* is rooted on string 3. Slide up or down the neck, placing the root on any letter named note, and you can play a power chord by that letter name. Playing only strings 1-2 results in a third possible shape—as a power chord dyad in the guitar's upper range. (In the higher range it is used less as a chord and more as a soloing dyad, nevertheless, it is technically still a power chord.)

Movable G5-form (1-3)   **Partial G5-form (1-4)**

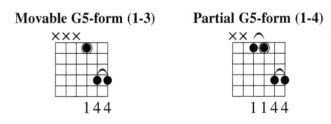

The following progression mixes the G5-form power chord shape with the D5-form. Memorize the note names on the third string now if you don't already know them. (See page 47.)

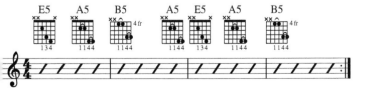

Suspensions are major or minor chords in which the 3rd tone has been replaced by either a 2nd or 4th. Suspended chords have a somewhat tense quality as the 2nd or 4th tone pulls to resolve to the 3rd. The *chord formula* for a suspended 2nd is 1–2–5, and a supended 4th is 1–4–5.

> Suspended 2nd: 1–2–5
> Suspended 4th: 1–4–5

Sus2 and sus4 chords may be played in each of the five forms, however, the most common shapes by far are the E-form, A-form, and D-form. So we will concentrate on these shapes. Again, each movable shape may be used to play any letter named chord.

If you are not already familiar with the basic major shapes (pages 6-10), it is highly recommended that you familiarize yourself with them first, as these sus2 and sus4 shapes should be seen as variations from the major forms.

> • Sus2 is sometimes used interchangably with add9 because the 2nd and the 9th tones are identical. However, technically, a sus2 chord has no 3rd while an add9 does contain the 3rd.

Suspended 2nd, E-form

The *sus2 E-form* barre chord is a suspended 2nd variation on the basic E-form shape. The root lies on the sixth string. Slide the entire shape up or down the neck, placing the root on any letter named note, and you can play a sus2 chord by that letter name.

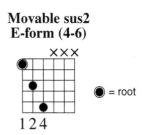

Movable sus2
E-form (4-6)

1 2 4

● = root

The sample progression below uses E-form sus2 chords. Play it with each of the shapes shown above.

> • Make sure you mute unwanted strings with the sides of your fretting fingers in order to eliminate all unwanted string noise.

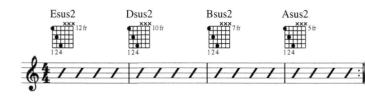

Esus2 Dsus2 Bsus2 Asus2

Suspended 2nd, A-form

The *sus2 A-form* barre chord is derived from the shape of the open Asus2 chord. The root lies on the fifth string. Slide the entire shape up or down the neck, placing the root on any letter named note, and you can play a sus2 chord by that letter name.

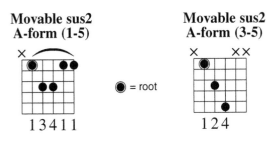

Movable sus2 A-form (1-5)

1 3 4 1 1

Movable sus2 A-form (3-5)

1 2 4

⬤ = root

Try the sample progression below with each of the A-form sus2 shapes above.

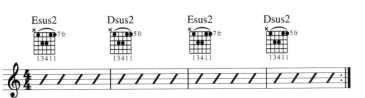

Suspended 2nd, D-form

The *sus2 D-form* barre chord resembles the shape of the open Dsus2 chord. The root lies on the fourth string. Slide the entire shape up or down the neck, placing the root on any letter named note, and you can play a sus2 chord by that letter name.

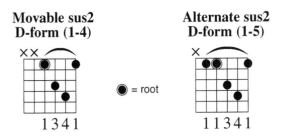

Movable sus2 D-form (1-4)

1 3 4 1

Alternate sus2 D-form (1-5)

1 1 3 4 1

⬤ = root

Try the sample progression below using the D-form shapes shown above.

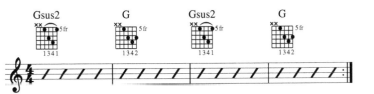

Suspended 4th, E-form

The *E-form sus4* barre chord is derived from the shape of the open Esus4 chord. The root lies on the sixth string.

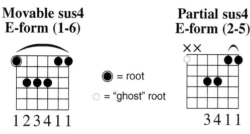

Movable sus4 E-form (1-6)

Partial sus4 E-form (2-5)

⬤ = root

◯ = "ghost" root

1 2 3 4 1 1

3 4 1 1

The progression below uses E-form sus4 shapes.

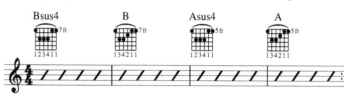

Bsus4	B	Asus4	A
7 fr	7 fr	5 fr	5 fr
1 2 3 4 1 1	1 3 4 2 1 1	1 2 3 4 1 1	1 3 4 2 1 1

Suspended 4th, A-form

The *A-form sus4* barre chord is derived from the shape of the open Asus4 chord. The root lies on the fifth string.

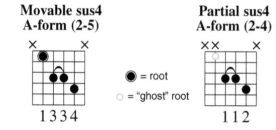

Movable sus4 A-form (2-5)

Partial sus4 A-form (2-4)

⬤ = root

◯ = "ghost" root

1 3 3 4

1 1 2

The progression below uses A-form sus2 shapes.

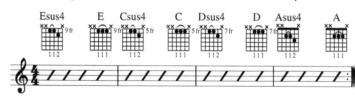

Esus4	E	Csus4	C	Dsus4	D	Asus4	A
9 fr	9 fr	5 fr	5 fr	7 fr	7 fr		
1 1 2	1 1 1	1 1 2	1 1 1	1 1 2	1 1 1	1 1 2	1 1 1

Suspended 4th, D-form

The *D-form sus4* barre chord is derived from the shape of the open Dsus4 chord. The root lies on the fourth string.

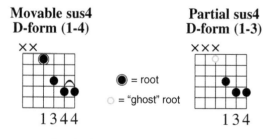

Movable sus4 D-form (1-4)

Partial sus4 D-form (1-3)

⬤ = root

◯ = "ghost" root

1 3 4 4

1 3 4

The progression below uses D-form sus4 shapes.

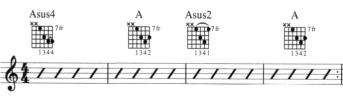

Asus4	A	Asus2	A
7 fr	7 fr	7 fr	7 fr
1 3 4 4	1 3 4 2	1 3 4 1	1 3 4 2

PART III
Seventh Chords

Seventh chords are major or minor chords onto which has been stacked another 3rd interval (on top of the 5th). This results in a four-tone chord containing a root, 3rd, 5th, and 7th. These chords are used in blues and jazz as well as other styles. There are four different kinds of seventh chords:

Dominant 7th:	1–3–5–♭7
Major 7th:	1–3–5–7
Minor 7th:	1–♭3–5–♭7
Minor (major 7th):	1–♭3–5–7

Dominant 7th chords are generally referred to as simply "7th" chords, and are the most common type. They consist of a major chord with an added ♭7th tone. Major 7th chords consist of a major chord with an added major 7th tone. Minor 7th chords consist of a minor chord with an added ♭7th tone. Finally, minor (major 7th) chords consist of a minor chord with an added major 7th tone. These are the least common of the bunch. Seventh chords may be played in each of the five forms. Again, each movable shape may be used to play any letter named chord.

If you are not already familiar with the basic major and minor shapes (pages 6-14), it is highly recommended that you familiarize yourself with them first, as these seventh chord shapes should be seen as variations on the original major shapes.

DOMINANT 7TH

Dominant 7th, E-form
The E-form dominant 7th barre chord is derived from the shape of the open E7 chord. Three common versions are shown below. The root lies on the sixth string.

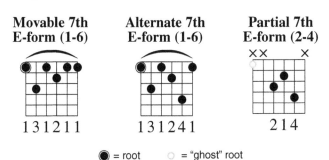

Movable 7th E-form (1-6)	**Alternate 7th E-form (1-6)**	**Partial 7th E-form (2-4)**
1 3 1 2 1 1	1 3 1 2 4 1	2 1 4

● = root   ○ = "ghost" root

The sample progression below uses E-form 7th chords. Play it with each of the shapes shown above.

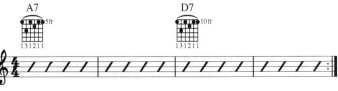

Dominant 7th, A-form

The A-form dominant 7th barre chord is derived from the shape of the open A7 chord. Three common movable shapes are shown below. The root lies on the fifth string. Slide the entire shape up or down the neck, placing the root on any letter named note, and you can play a 7th chord by that letter name.

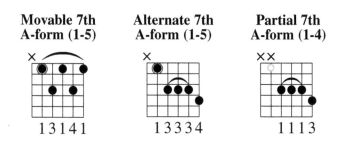

Movable 7th
A-form (1-5)

1 3 1 4 1

Alternate 7th
A-form (1-5)

1 3 3 3 4

Partial 7th
A-form (1-4)

1 1 1 3

Try the sample progression below with each of the A-form 7th chord shapes above.

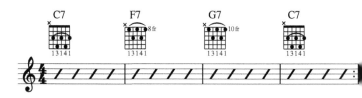

Dominant 7th, D-form

The D-form dominant 7th barre chord is derived from the shape of the open D7 chord. The root lies on the fourth string. Slide the entire shape up or down the neck, placing the root on any letter named note, and you can play a 7th chord by that letter name.

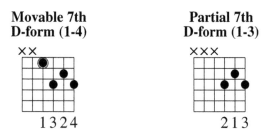

Movable 7th
D-form (1-4)

1 3 2 4

Partial 7th
D-form (1-3)

2 1 3

Try the sample progression below with each the D-form 7th chord shapes shown above.

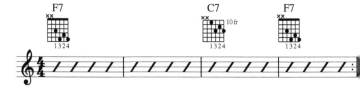

Dominant 7th, C-form

The C-form dominant 7th barre chord is derived from the shape of the open C7 chord. The root lies on the fifth string. Slide the entire shape up or down the neck, placing the root on any letter named note, and you can play a 7th chord by that letter name.

> • Not every tone of a chord is always included in every chord shape. These, for example, omit the 5th of the chord.

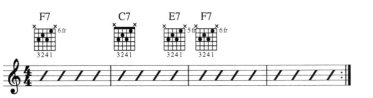

Movable 7th
C-form (2-5)

3 2 4 1

Partial 7th
C-form (3-5)

2 1 3

Try the sample progression below with each of the C-form 7th chord shapes above.

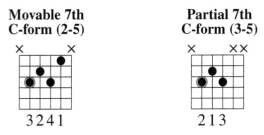

F7
3 2 4 1

C7
3 2 4 1

E7
3 2 4 1

F7
3 2 4 1

Dominant 7th, G-form

The G-form dominant 7th barre chord is a variation of the major G-form shape. The root lies on the sixth string. Slide the entire shape up or down the neck, placing the root on any letter named note, and you can play a 7th chord by that letter name.

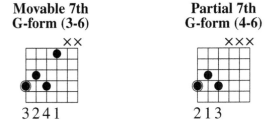

Movable 7th
G-form (3-6)

3 2 4 1

Partial 7th
G-form (4-6)

2 1 3

Try the sample progression below with each the G-form 7th chord shapes shown above.

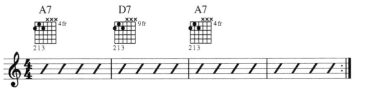

A7
2 1 3

D7
2 1 3

A7
2 1 3

Major 7th, E-form

The E-form major 7th barre chord is derived from the open Emaj7 shape. The root lies on the sixth string. Slide the entire shape up or down the neck, placing the root on any letter named note, and you can play a major 7th chord by that letter name.

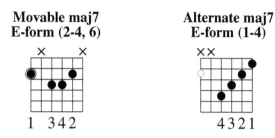

Movable maj7 E-form (2-4, 6)

1 342

Alternate maj7 E-form (1-4)

4 3 2 1

Try the sample progression below with each of the E-form major 7th chord shapes shown above.

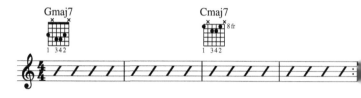

Gmaj7
1 342

Cmaj7
8 fr
1 342

Major 7th, A-form

The A-form major 7th barre chord is derived from the shape of the open Amaj7 chord. Three movable shapes are shown below. The root lies on the fifth string. Slide the entire shape up or down the neck, placing the root on any letter named note, and you can play a major 7th chord by that letter name.

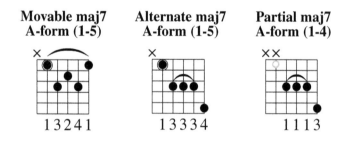

Movable maj7 A-form (1-5)

1 3 2 4 1

Alternate maj7 A-form (1-5)

1 3 3 3 4

Partial maj7 A-form (1-4)

1 1 1 3

Try the sample progression below with each of the A-form major 7th chord shapes above.

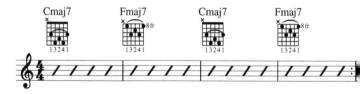

Cmaj7
1 3 2 4 1

Fmaj7
8 fr
1 3 2 4 1

Cmaj7
1 3 2 4 1

Fmaj7
8 fr
1 3 2 4 1

Major 7th, D-form

The D-form major 7th barre chord is derived from the shape of the open Dmaj7 chord. The root lies on the fourth string.

Movable maj7
D-form (1-4)

1 3 3 3

The progression below uses D-form major 7th shapes.

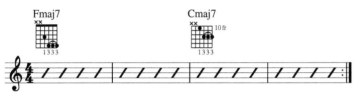

Major 7th, C-form

The C-form major 7th barre chord is derived from the shape of the open Cmaj7 chord. The root lies on the fifth string.

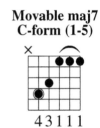

Movable maj7
C-form (1-5)

4 3 1 1 1

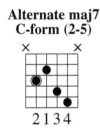

Alternate maj7
C-form (2-5)

2 1 3 4

The progression below uses C-form major 7th shapes.

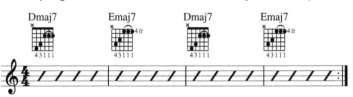

Major 7th, G-form

The G-form major 7th barre chord is a variation of the major G-form shape. The root lies on the sixth string.

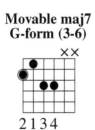

Movable maj7
G-form (3-6)

2 1 3 4

The progression below uses G-form major 7th shapes.

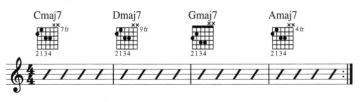

Minor 7th, E-form

The E-form minor 7th barre chord is derived from the open Em7 shape. The root lies on the sixth string. Slide the entire shape up or down the neck, placing the root on any letter named note, and you can play a minor 7th chord by that letter name.

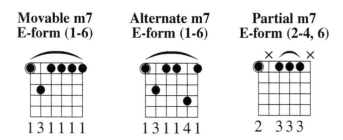

Try the sample progression below with each of the E-form minor 7th chord shapes shown above.

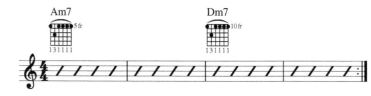

Minor 7th, A-form

The A-form minor 7th barre chord is derived from the shape of the open Am7 chord. The root lies on the fifth string. Slide the entire shape up or down the neck, placing the root on any letter named note, and you can play a minor 7th chord by that letter name.

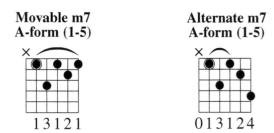

Try the sample progression below with each of the A-form minor 7th chord shapes above.

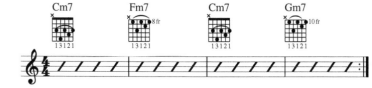

Minor 7th, D-form

The D-form minor 7th barre chord is derived from the shape of the open Dm7 chord. The root lies on the fourth string.

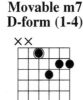

Movable m7
D-form (1-4)

1 4 2 3

The progression below uses D-form minor 7th shapes.

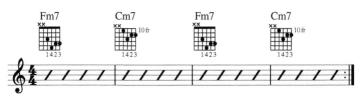

Minor 7th, C-form

The C-form minor 7th barre chord is a variation of the dominant 7th shape. The root lies on the fifth string.

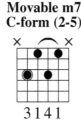

Movable m7
C-form (2-5)

3 1 4 1

The progression below uses C-form minor 7th shapes.

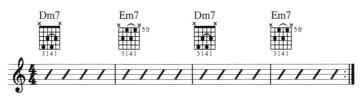

Minor 7th, G-form

The G-form minor 7th barre chord is a variation of the major G-form shape. The root lies on the sixth string.

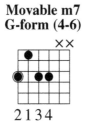

Movable m7
G-form (4-6)

2 1 3 4

The progression below uses G-form minor 7th shapes.

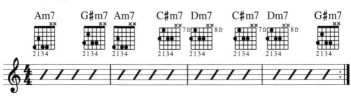

Minor (major 7th), E-form

The E-form minor (major 7th) barre chord is a variation on the minor E-form. The root lies on the sixth string. Slide the entire shape up or down the neck, placing the root on any letter named note, and you can play a minor (major 7th) chord by that letter name.

- Lightly touch and mute string 5 with the side of your index finger in order to eliminate unwanted string noise.

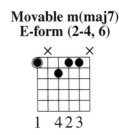

Movable m(maj7)
E-form (2-4, 6)

1 4 2 3

Try the sample progression below using the E-form minor (major 7th) chord shape.

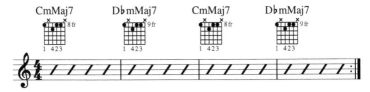

Minor (major 7th), A-form

The A-form minor (major 7th) barre chord is a variation on the minor A-form. The root lies on the fifth string. Slide the entire shape up or down the neck, placing the root on any letter named note, and you can play a minor (major 7th) chord by that letter name.

- Lightly touch and mute string 4 with the side of your index finger in order to eliminate unwanted string noise.

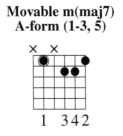

Movable m(maj7)
A-form (1-3, 5)

1 3 4 2

Try the sample progression below using the A-form minor (major 7th) chord shape.

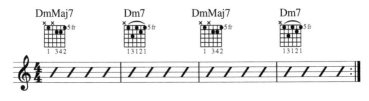

Minor (major 7th), D-form

The D-form minor (major 7th) barre chord is a variation on the minor D-form. The root lies on the fourth string.

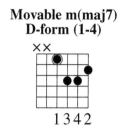

Movable m(maj7)
D-form (1-4)

1 3 4 2

Practice the D-form minor (major 7th) shape below.

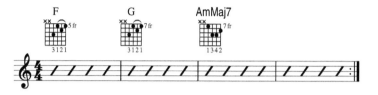

Minor (major 7th), C-form

The C-form minor (major 7th) barre chord is a variation on the minor C-form. The root lies on the fifth string.

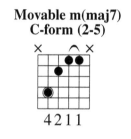

Movable m(maj7)
C-form (2-5)

4 2 1 1

Practice the C-form minor (major 7th) shape below.

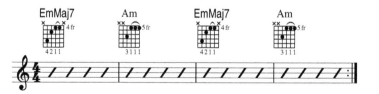

PART IV
Ninth Chords

Ninth chords are seventh chords onto which has been stacked another 3rd interval (on top of the 7th). This results in a five-tone chord containing a root, 3rd, 5th, 7th, and 9th. These chords are used in blues and jazz as well as other styles. There are three basic types of ninth chords:

Dominant 9th: $1\text{–}3\text{–}5\text{–}\flat7\text{–}9$
Major 9th: $1\text{–}3\text{–}5\text{–}7\text{–}9$
Minor 9th: $1\text{–}\flat3\text{–}5\text{–}\flat7\text{–}9$

Dominant 9th chords are generally referred to as simply "9th" chords, and are the most common type. They consist of a dominant 7th chord with an added 9th tone. Major 9th chords consist of a major 7th chord with an added 9th tone. Minor 9th chords consist of a minor 7th chord with an added 9th tone. Ninth chords may be played using a number of different forms. Again, any movable shape may be used to play any letter-named chord.

If you are not already familiar with the 7th chord shapes (pages 21-29), it is recommended that you familiarize yourself with them first, as these ninth chord shapes can be seen as variations on the 7th chords they are built from.

DOMINANT 9TH

Dominant 9th, E-form

The *E-form dominant 9th* barre chord is shown below in two versions. (Alternatively, you could also view the second one as being a D-form.) The root lies on the sixth string. Slide the entire shape up or down the neck, placing the root on any letter named note, and you can play a 9th chord by that letter name.

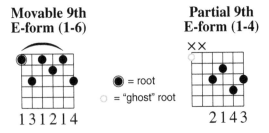

**Movable 9th
E-form (1-6)**

⬤ = root
○ = "ghost" root

**Partial 9th
E-form (1-4)**

The sample progression below uses E-form dominant 9th chords. Play it using both of the shapes above.

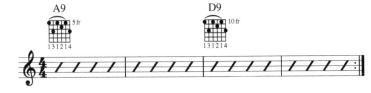

Dominant 9th, A-form

The *A-form dominant 9th* barre chord is shown below. The root is on the fifth string. (Actually, this shape has no third and therefore could function as either a dominant 9th or a minor 9th. It is ambiguous.)

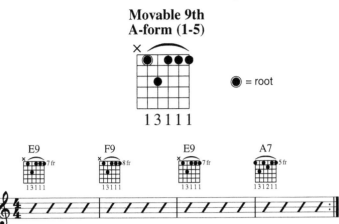

Dominant 9th, C-form

The *C-form dominant 9th* barre chord is the probably the most common form. The root is on the fifth string.

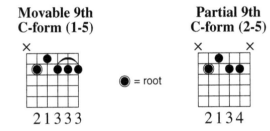

Try the sample progression below with each of the A-form dominant 9th shapes above.

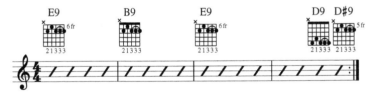

Dominant 9th, G-form

The *G-form dominant 9th* barre chord is perhaps the second most commonly used form, after the C-form. The root lies on the sixth string.

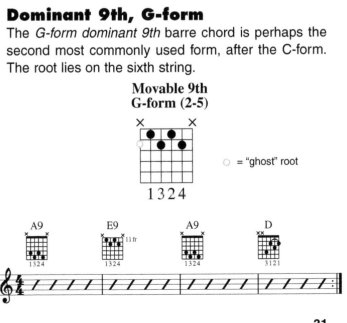

Major 9th, E-form

The *E-form major 9th* barre chords are shown below. The root lies on the sixth string.

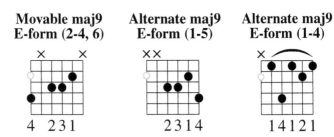

Movable maj9 E-form (2-4, 6)   **Alternate maj9 E-form (1-5)**   **Alternate maj9 E-form (1-4)**

4   2 3 1   2 3 1 4   1 4 1 2 1

Try the sample progression below using each of the E-form major 9th chord shapes shown above.

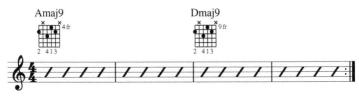

Amaj9   Dmaj9

Major 9th, C-form

The *C-form major 9th* barre chords are shown below. The root lies on the fifth string.

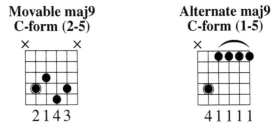

Movable maj9 C-form (2-5)   **Alternate maj9 C-form (1-5)**

2 1 4 3   4 1 1 1 1

Try the sample progression below using each of the C-form major 9th chord shapes shown above.

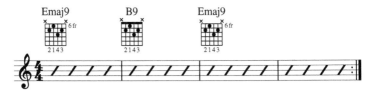

Emaj9   B9   Emaj9

Major 9th, G-form

The *G-form major 9th* barre chords are shown below. The root lies on the sixth string.

Movable maj9 G-form (1-4)

1 3 1 4

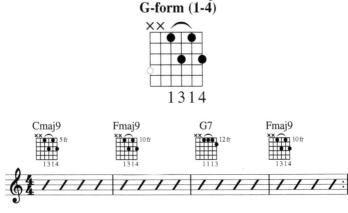

Cmaj9   Fmaj9   G7   Fmaj9

Minor 9th, E-form

The *E-form minor 9th* barre chords are shown below in full and partial versions. Notice the similarity to the E-form minor 7th shape. The root lies on the sixth string.

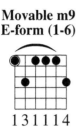

Movable m9
E-form (1-6)

1 3 1 1 1 4

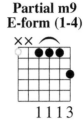

Partial m9
E-form (1-4)

1 1 1 3

Try the sample progression below using each of the E-form minor 9th chord shapes shown above.

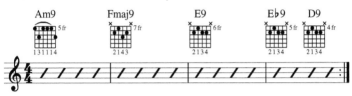

Minor 9th, C-form

The *C-form minor 9th* barre chords are shown below. The root lies on the fifth string.

Movable m9
C-form (2-5)

2 1 3 3 3

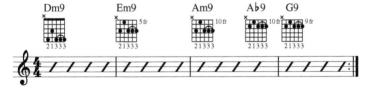

Minor 9th, G-form

The *G-form minor 9th* barre chords are shown below. The root lies on the sixth string.

Movable m9
G-form (2-4, 6)

1 3 4 2

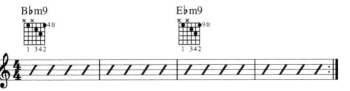

33

PART V
Added Tones

Added chords are the result of taking a major or minor chord and simply adding an extra tone. Here, we will look at five such chords.

Added 9th:	1–3–5–9
Minor added 9th:	1–♭3–5–9
6th:	1–3–5–6
Minor 6th:	1–♭3–5–6
6th added 9th:	1–3–5–6–9

If you are not already familiar with the major and minor chord shapes (pages 6-14), it is recommended that you familiarize yourself with them first, as these added chord shapes can be seen as variations on the major and minor shapes.

ADDED 9TH

E-form, A-form, D-form, & G-form

The most common *added 9th* barre chords are shown below. Notice that the A-form and D-form shapes were also previously shown as sus2 chords. These shapes may also appear labelled as add9, although in so labelling them we are implying that the third of the chord is included—or could be included—even if it is not actually played. Slide each shape up or down the neck, placing its root on any letter named note, and you can play an added 9th chord by that letter name.

Movable add9 E-form (1-4)

3 2 1 4

Movable add9 A-form (1-5)

1 3 4 1 1

Movable add9 D-form (1-5)

1 1 3 4 1

Movable add9 G-form (1-4)

1 3 1 4

• The progression below uses add9 chords. Substitute the various shapes above and notice how the leading melody tones change.

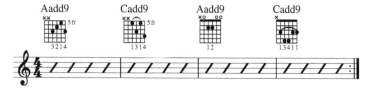

E-form

The three *E-form minor added 9th* barre chords are shown below. Slide each shape up or down the neck, placing its root on any letter named note, and you can play a minor added 9th chord by that letter name.

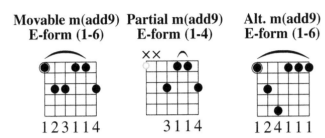

Movable m(add9)
E-form (1-6)
1 2 3 1 1 4

Partial m(add9)
E-form (1-4)
3 1 1 4

Alt. m(add9)
E-form (1-6)
1 2 4 1 1 1

Check out the sample progression below with each of the three minor added 9th shown above.

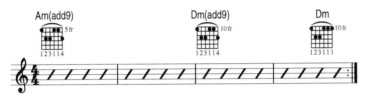

Am(add9)   5 fr   123114

Dm(add9)   10 fr   123114

Dm   10 fr   123111

A-form, D-form, C-form

The remaining *minor added 9th* barre chords are shown below. Slide each shape up or down the neck, placing its root on any letter named note, and you can play a minor added 9th chord by that letter name.

- The A-form m(add9) is particularly difficult in the lower frets, but works well in the upper range.

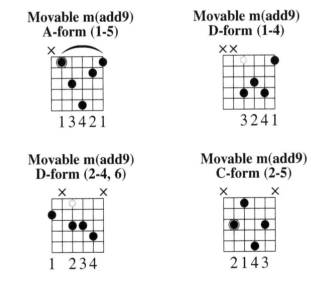

Movable m(add9)
A-form (1-5)
1 3 4 2 1

Movable m(add9)
D-form (1-4)
3 2 4 1

Movable m(add9)
D-form (2-4, 6)
1 2 3 4

Movable m(add9)
C-form (2-5)
2 1 4 3

The sample progression below uses E-form added 9th chords. Substitute the other shapes above as well.

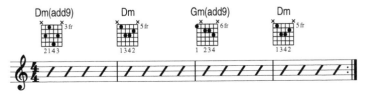

Dm(add9)   3 fr   2143

Dm   5 fr   1342

Gm(add9)   6 fr   1 234

Dm   5 fr   1342

E-form

A 6th chord is a major chord with an added 6th tone. Two *E-form 6th* barre chords are shown below. Slide each shape up or down the neck, placing its root on any letter named note, and you can play a 6th chord by that letter name.

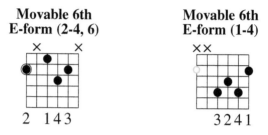

Try the sample progression below with each of the 6th chord shapes shown above.

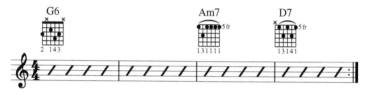

A-form, D-form, C-form

The remaining *6th* barre chords are shown below. Slide each shape up or down the neck, placing its root on any letter named note, and you can play a 6th chord by that letter name.

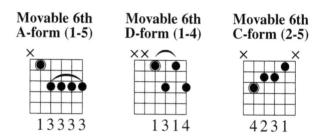

The sample progression below uses 6th chords. Try it with each of the forms shown above.

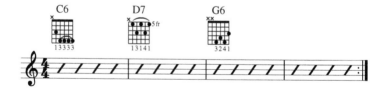

E-form

A minor 6th chord is a minor chord with an added 6th tone. Two *E-form minor 6th* barre chords are shown below. Slide each shape up or down the neck, placing its root on any letter named note, and you can play a minor 6th chord by that letter name.

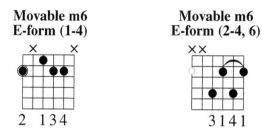

Movable m6
E-form (1-4)

2 1 3 4

Movable m6
E-form (2-4, 6)

3 1 4 1

Try the sample progression below with each of the minor 6th chord shapes shown above.

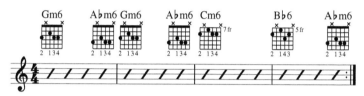

A-form, D-form, C-form

The remaining *minor 6th* barre chords are shown below. Slide each shape up or down the neck, placing its root on any letter named note, and you can play a minor 6th chord by that letter name.

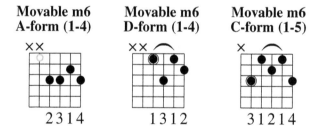

Movable m6
A-form (1-4)

2 3 1 4

Movable m6
D-form (1-4)

1 3 1 2

Movable m6
C-form (1-5)

3 1 2 1 4

The sample progression below uses minor 6th chords. Try it with each of the forms shown above.

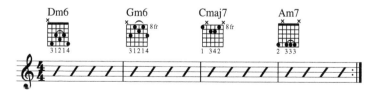

E-form, A-form, C-form

The *6th added 9th* barre chords are shown below in four different versions.

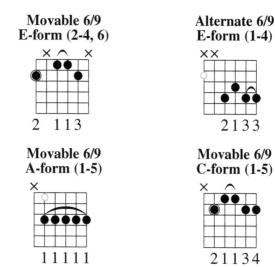

The sample progression below uses 6th added 9th chords. Try it using each of the shapes above.

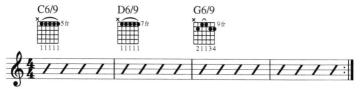

E-form, A-form, C-form

The *minor 6th added 9th* barre chord are shown below in four different versions.

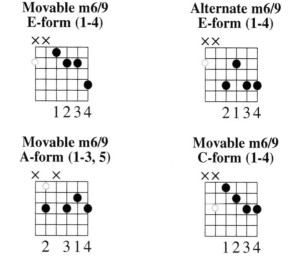

The sample progression below uses minor 6th added 9th chords. Try it using each of the shapes above.

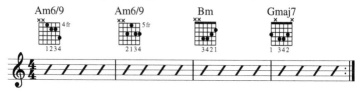

PART VI
Altered Tones

This section covers a number of chords that include various altered tones, such as 7♭5, 7♭9, and 7sus4 chords. The chord formulas for these types are:

7th flatted 5th:	1–3–♭5–♭7
7th flatted 9th:	1–3–5–♭7–♭9
7th sharped 9th:	1–3–5–♭7–♯9
7th suspended 4th:	1–4–5–♭7

If you are not already familiar with the 7th chord shapes (pages 21-29), it is recommended that you familiarize yourself with them first, as these alterations can be seen as variations on the basic 7th chords.

7TH FLATTED 5TH

All forms

The *7th flatted 5th* chord is like a dominant 7th chord but with a ♭5th instead of a perfect 5th. Below, it is shown in six different versions. Slide the entire shape up or down the neck, placing the root on any letter named note, and you can play a 7♭5 chord by that letter name.

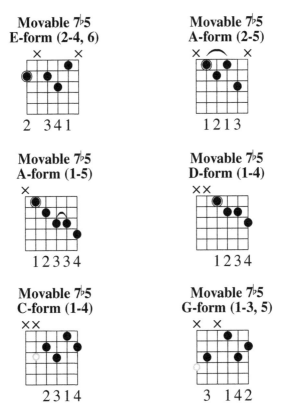

Try the sample progression below using each of the 7♭5 shapes above.

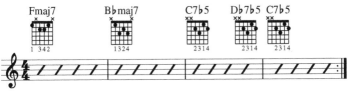

All forms

The *7th flatted 9th* chord is a dominant 7th chord with an added ♭9th tone. It is also very similar to the diminished 7th chord (page 42). In fact, if the root note of the 7b9 chord is omitted, it becomes a diminished 7th. Four movable shapes are shown below. Try the sample progression using each of them.

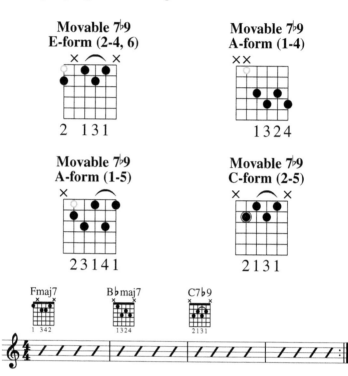

Movable 7♭9
E-form (2-4, 6)

2 1 3 1

Movable 7♭9
A-form (1-4)

1 3 2 4

Movable 7♭9
A-form (1-5)

2 3 1 4 1

Movable 7♭9
C-form (2-5)

2 1 3 1

Fmaj7   B♭maj7   C7♭9
1 342   1324   2131

7TH SHARPED 9TH

All forms

The *7th sharped 9th* chord is another tense chord made up of a dominant 7th chord with an added ♯9th tone. Although the #9th is the same pitch as the minor 3rd, in this case, the chord's major 3rd is employed (usually in the lower octave) and the #9th is heard to clash against it. Three movable shapes are shown below. Try the sample progression using each of them.

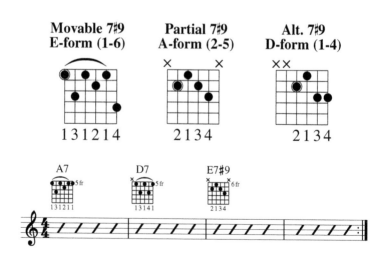

Movable 7♯9
E-form (1-6)

1 3 1 2 1 4

Partial 7♯9
A-form (2-5)

2 1 3 4

Alt. 7♯9
D-form (1-4)

2 1 3 4

A7   D7   E7♯9
5 fr   5 fr   6 fr
131211   13141   2134

E-form, A-form

The *E-form* and *A-form 7th suspended 4th* barre chords are shown below. Notice the similarity to the dominant 7th shapes. The roots lie on the sixth and fifth strings, respectively.

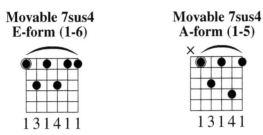

Try the sample progression below using both of the 7sus4 chord shapes above.

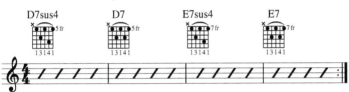

D-form, C-form

The *D-form* and *C-form 7th suspended 4th* barre chords are shown below. Again, notice the similarity to the dominant 7th shapes. The only difference is that the 3rd has been raised a half step to become a 4th. The root can be found on the fourth and fifth strings, respectively.

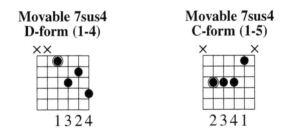

Try the sample progression below using both of the 7sus4 chord shapes above.

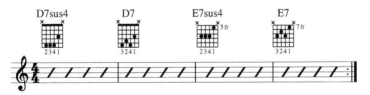

PART VII
Diminished and Augmented

Diminished chords are three note chords (triads) with a minor 3rd and diminished 5th tone. The Diminished 7th is a diminished triad with a double-flatted 7th tone (same pitch as the 6th).

Diminished: 1–♭3–♭5
Diminished 7th: 1–♭3–♭5–♭♭7

Diminished, All forms

Two *diminished* barre chords are shown below. The following sample progression incorporates both shapes.

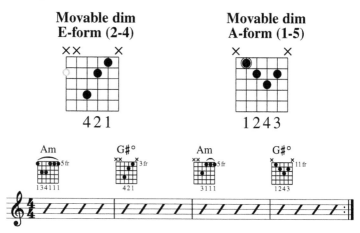

Diminished 7th, All forms

The *diminished 7th* barre chords are shown below.

- Diminished 7th chords can be shifted freely up or down the neck in three fret intervals without changing the chord name—only the inversion changes. Another characteristic is that any note within each dim7 chord may be considered as the root.

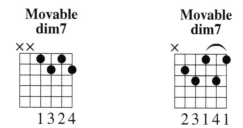

The sample progression below uses a dim7 in several inversions.

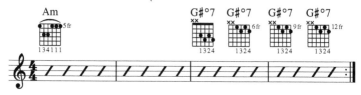

All forms

The *half diminished* chord is also known as a *minor 7th flatted 5th.* In other words, it is a diminished 7th chord in which the 7th is flatted only once (not a double flat). The chord formula is: $1\text{-}\flat3\text{-}\flat5\text{-}\flat7$

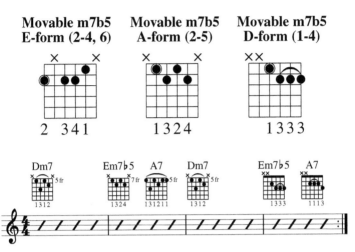

Movable m7b5 E-form (2-4, 6)   **Movable m7b5 A-form (2-5)**   **Movable m7b5 D-form (1-4)**

2 341   1324   1333

Dm7   Em7b5   A7   Dm7   Em7b5   A7

Augmented, Augmented 7th, All forms

Several augmented and augmented 7th shapes are shown below. Try each in the progression that follows.

- Similar to the diminished 7th, the augmented chords may be shifted freely up or down the neck in four-fret intervals, changing only the inversion.

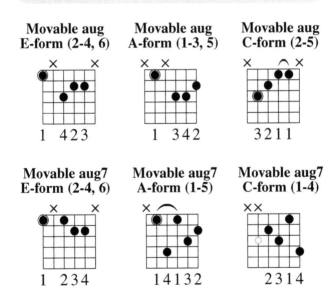

Movable aug E-form (2-4, 6)   **Movable aug A-form (1-3, 5)**   **Movable aug C-form (2-5)**

1 423   1 342   3211

Movable aug7 E-form (2-4, 6)   **Movable aug7 A-form (1-5)**   **Movable aug7 C-form (1-4)**

1 234   14132   2314

Use each augmented and augmented 7th shape above in place of the augmented chords below.

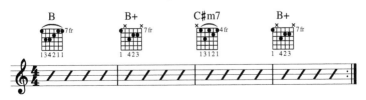

B   B+   C#m7   B+

DOMINANT 11TH (9SUS4)

All forms

The *dominant 11th* chord is generally considered too "harsh" as its major 3rd clashes strongly against the 11th (4th) tone. Therefore, the 3rd is omitted, which results in a *9th suspended 4th* chord. Still it is often written as an 11th. Technically, the chord formula for a true 11th chord is: 1–3–5–♭7–9–11. For a 9sus4, it is 1–4–5–♭7–9, with the 4th acting as the 11th tone.

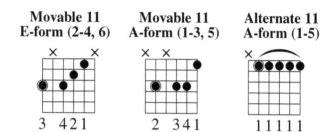

Movable 11 E-form (2-4, 6)	Movable 11 A-form (1-3, 5)	Alternate 11 A-form (1-5)
3 4 2 1	2 3 4 1	1 1 1 1 1

Substitute each of the 11th (9sus4) shapes above in the following progression.

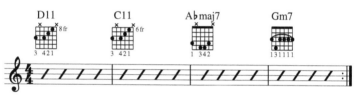

D11   C11   A♭maj7   Gm7

MINOR 11TH

All forms

The *minor 11th* chord doesn't have the same trouble as its dominant 11th counterpart. The chord formula for a minor 11th is: 1–♭3–5–♭7–9–11. Try out each of the following forms in the sample progression below.

Movable m11 E-form (2-4, 6)	Movable m11 A-form (1-5)	Alternate m11 A-form (1-3, 5)
2 3 4 1	1 1 1 2 1	2 3 4 1

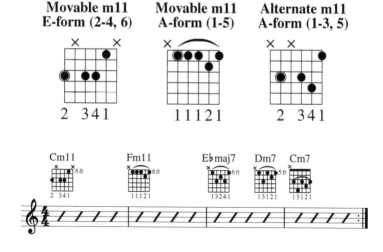

Cm11   Fm11   E♭maj7   Dm7   Cm7

All forms

The *dominant 13th* chord is generally referred to as simply a "13th." It consists of an 11th chord with yet another 3rd interval stacked on top. The 13th tone is actually the same as the 6th tone. The chord formula for a dominant 13th is: $1–3–5–\flat7–9–11–13$.

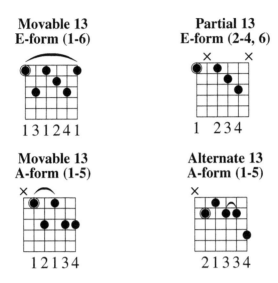

Movable 13
E-form (1-6)

1 3 1 2 4 1

Partial 13
E-form (2-4, 6)

1   2 3 4

Movable 13
A-form (1-5)

1 2 1 3 4

Alternate 13
A-form (1-5)

2 1 3 3 4

Substitute each of the 13th shapes above in the sample progression below.

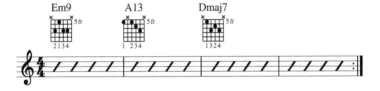

Em9   A13   Dmaj7

Appendix

Chord Construction Table

The table below shows the chord tones for each chord covered in this book.

Chord name	Abbreviation	Chord formula
major	(none)	1 3 5
minor	m	1 ♭3 5
power chord	5	1 5
suspended 2nd	sus2	1 2 5
suspended 4th	sus4	1 4 5
dominant 7th	7th	1 3 5 ♭7
major 7th	maj7	1 3 5 7
minor 7th	m7	1 ♭3 5 ♭7
minor (major 7th)	m(maj7)	1 ♭3 5 7
dominant 9th	9	1 3 5 ♭7 9
major 9th	maj9	1 3 5 7 9
minor 9th	m9	1 ♭3 5 ♭7 9
added 9th	add9	1 3 5 9
minor added 9th	m(add9)	1 ♭3 5 9
6th	6	1 3 5 6
minor 6th	m6	1 ♭3 5 6
6th added 9th	6/9	1 3 5 6 9
minor 6th added 9th	m6/9	1 ♭3 5 6 9
7th flatted 5th	7♭5	1 3 ♭5 ♭7
7th flatted 9th	7♭9	1 3 5 ♭7 ♭9
7th sharped 9th	7♯9	1 3 5 ♭7 ♯9
7th suspended 4th	7sus4	1 4 5 ♭7
diminished	o	1 ♭3 ♭5
diminished 7th	o7	1 ♭3 ♭5 ♭♭7
half diminished	ø	1 ♭3 ♭5 ♭7
minor 7th flatted 5th	m7♭5	1 ♭3 ♭5 ♭7
Augmented	+	1 3 ♯5
Augmented 7th	+7	1 3 ♯5 ♭7
dominant 11th	11	1 3 5 ♭7 9 11
9th suspended 4th	9sus4	1 4 5 ♭7 9
minor 11th	m11	1 ♭3 5 ♭7 9 11
dominant 13th	13	1 3 5 ♭7 9 11 13

Note Names on the Neck

The vertical lines below represent the guitar strings, and the horizontal lines represent the frets. The low E string is on the left; the high E string on the right. The frets between the labeled notes are named with either a sharp of the note right below it (in terms of pitch), or a flat of the note right above it.

To play a particular chord using any movable shape found in this book, simply note which string the movable chord's root is on. Then find the appropriate letter-named note on the correct string in the diagram below, and form the chord shape at that fret. To play a different letter-named chord using that same shape, simply slide the entire pattern up or down the neck to move the root to the new position.

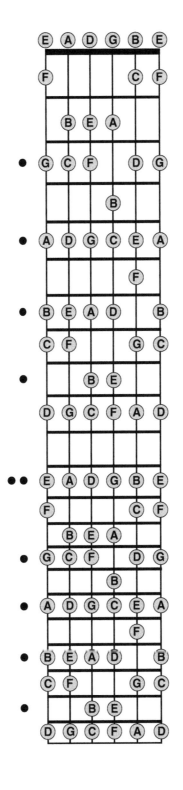